**Contents**

GW01048675

About this book with
Foreword by Archbishop Vincent Nichols (Westminster)

Hail, Mary   6
Group session on relating to Mary

Full of grace   10
Group session on Mary as 'the New Eve'

The Lord is with thee   15
Group session on Mary, 'uncertainty and suffering'

Blessed art thou amongst women   20
Group session on Mary and her trust in God

Blessed is the fruit of thy womb   24
Group session on Mary as the bearer of the Word of God

Holy Mary, Mother of God, pray for us sinners   28
Group session on Mary as mother and intercessor

Daily Prayers   33
Prayers from Sunday to Saturday

Supplementary resources including   48
Shrines, quotes, prayers, documents and Mary in the Church's Year

Nihil Obstat: Father Anton Cowan, Censor
Imprimatur: The Most Reverend Vincent Nichols, Archbishop of Westminster
Date: Feast of the Assumption of the Blessed Virgin Mary 15 August 2010

The Nihil obstat *and* Imprimatur *are a declaration that a book or pamphlet is considered to be free from doctrinal or moral error. It is not implied that those who have granted the* Nihil obstat *and* Imprimatur *agree with the contents, opinions or statements expressed.*

Writing Group: Dr Mark Nash, Fr Michael O'Boy, Mrs Margaret Wickware

The Westminster Diocesan Agency for Evangelisation is grateful to the National Council of the Churches of Christ in the U.S.A for use of the New Revised Standard Version Bible: Catholic Edition copyright © 1993 and 1989. Extracts from The Catechism of the Catholic Church are reproduced by kind permission of the Continuum International Publishing Group. Excerpts from The Divine Office © 1974, hierarchies of Australia, England and Wales, Ireland. All rights reserved.

This booklet contains images from wendyryanfolkart.blogspot.com, pictures of Westminster Cathedral mosaic and images freely available via the Wikimedia Commons website.

Produced by Agency for Evangelisation, Vaughan House, 46 Francis Street, London, SW1P 1QN. Tel: 020 7798 9152; email: evangelisation@rcdow.org.uk

 booklets are published by WRCDT. Design by Mark Nash. Printing by Buckland Press Ltd www.buckland.co.uk.

Full of Grace

Foreword

For someone so central to the Christian drama, there is relatively little about Mary in the Scriptures. Other early Christian texts, such as the infancy narratives of James and Thomas, seek to fill in the detail, but in Scripture Mary stands very much in the background. But we know that Mary treasures and ponders in her heart all that is said about and by her son (Luke 2). In this we follow in her footsteps. We too seek an understanding of and intimacy with Christ. In her journey of faith to her eternal credit, she travelled always and everywhere in hope. We are called to do the same.

Occasionally, as at the Annunciation (Luke 1:26-38) or the wedding feast at Cana (John 2:1-12), Mary's voice breaks through into Scripture. When she speaks, it is not to claim a position or rights for herself. Rather, it is to praise the God who has done great things for her, to remind us that He will do great things for us, and to point us to Christ. 'Do whatever he tells you', she commands the servants at the wedding feast (John 2:5)

Mary's reticence, her humility, is not to be confused with that of the weak-kneed or simpering. In her silence we find a wealth of courage. Courage to let go of whatever plans she had for her own life, courage to endure where friends and family may have ridiculed her, and where, in the final stages, even the disciples walked away.

Silence can mean many things. Depending on the situation it can be a signal of affirmation or protest. It can be a welcome respite from the noise of the day or an uneasy truce. It can be a familiar understanding between friends or an embarassing gulf between strangers. For Mary, silence was the place in which she grew in love of God. And in her silence, despite the trials and suffering she encountered, Mary remained altogether faithful. As we reflect on her life and rejoice in her discipleship, may we be drawn closer to her Son, opening ourselves to the invitation 'to Jesus, through Mary'.

Yours devotedly,

+ Vincent Nichols

The Most Reverend Vincent Nichols
Archbishop of Westminster

Hail Mary
Full of Grace

About this book

Some two thousand years ago came the turning point of all human history. God, who again and again offered a covenant to man (*Eucharistic Prayer IV*), gave his definitive gift to humankind, Jesus Christ, conceived by the power of the Holy Spirit and born of the Virgin Mary. This booklet on Mary is to be understood in these terms; for 'what the Catholic faith believes about Mary is based on what it believes about Christ, and what it teaches about Mary illumines in turn its faith in Christ' (*Catechism of the Catholic Church*, 487).

The *Hail, Mary*, which we are taught as children, which lies at the heart of the Rosary and the Angelus, and which many parishes say together on a Sunday, forms the structure of this resource. In the six group sessions we will explore what the Scriptures and the Church say about Mary - the immaculately conceived, sinless, ever-virgin, mother of Christ, assumed into heaven.

The group sessions are supplemented by additional materials and text boxes on Church documents, prayers and shrines which serve to illustrate the centuries old tradition of prayer through Our Lady. Such devotions which have built up over the years can help develop the 'habits of virtue' such as 'patience, acceptance of the Cross in daily life and a spirit of ready service' (*General Directory of Catechesis*, 195). As it is often through art that many first encounter Our Lady we have made use of icons, traditional painting and contemporary art. While these illustrate the text, they also serve an additional purpose of inviting the reader and their group to pause and reflect. We also invite you to make use of the daily prayers in the second half of the booklet which are drawn from the Divine Office.

This booklet is not tied to a particular time of year and would be ideal for groups seeking to meet together, for example, on a particular Marian feast. Additional reflections and thoughts can be found on our small group blog (dowsmallgroups. wordpress.com). We pray that this resource and your time together helps you to grow in faith and love, with each other and with Jesus Christ, by better understanding Mary, our 'outstanding model in faith and charity' (*Lumen Gentium*, 53).

Hail Mary
Full of Grace

The Birth of Christ by Franz von Rohden (1853)

Hail Mary
Full of Grace

Hail, Mary

Opening Prayers

Taken from the book of the Prophet Isaiah 61:9-11

Leader: Their descendants shall be known among the nations,
and their offspring among the peoples;
all who see them shall acknowledge
that they are a people whom the Lord has blessed.

Group: I will greatly rejoice in the Lord,
my whole being shall exult in my God;
for he has clothed me with the garments of salvation,

Leader: he has covered me with the robe of righteousness,
as a bridegroom decks himself with a garland,
and as a bride adorns herself with her jewels.

Group: For as the earth brings forth its shoots,
and as a garden causes what is sown in it to spring up,
so the Lord God will cause righteousness and praise
to spring up before all the nations.

All: Glory be to the Father, and to the Son and to the Holy Spirit. As it was in
the beginning, is now, and ever shall be, world without end. Amen.

*For a few moments, either aloud or in the silence of our hearts, let us give thanks to
the Lord for all the blessings we have received over the past week. As we give thanks
let us remember, again in silence or aloud, all those who need our prayers. The word
repent means to turn around - keeping in mind God's mercy, let us remember all the
times that we have turned from him and ask for his forgiveness.*

Introduction to the Scripture reading

St. Matthew wrote: 'Ask and it will be given to you; search, and you will find; knock
and the door will be opened for you.' Let us now, with trust in the Father, seek
his will in reading, find it in meditating; knock in mental prayer for an opening to
God's love and wisdom through sharing and contemplation.

After Matthew 7:7 and Guido the Carthusian

Hail Mary
Full of Grace

Explore the Scriptures Luke 1:26-38

In the sixth month the angel Gabriel was sent by God to a town in Galilee called Nazareth, to a virgin engaged to a man whose name was Joseph, of the house of David. The virgin's name was Mary. And he came to her and said, 'Rejoice, so highly favoured! The Lord is with you.' But she was much perplexed by his words and pondered what sort of greeting this might be.

The angel said to her, 'Do not be afraid, Mary, for you have found favour with God. And now, you will conceive in your womb and bear a son, and you will name him Jesus. He will be great, and will be called the Son of the Most High, and the Lord God will give to him the throne of his ancestor David. He will reign over the house of Jacob for ever, and of his kingdom there will be no end.' Mary said to the angel, 'How can this be, since I am a virgin?'

The angel said to her, 'The Holy Spirit will come upon you, and the power of the Most High will overshadow you; therefore the child to be born will be holy; he will be called Son of God. And now, your relative Elizabeth in her old age has also conceived a son; and this is the sixth month for her who was said to be barren. For nothing will be impossible with God.' Then Mary said, 'Here am I, the servant of the Lord; let it be with me according to your word.' Then the angel departed from her.

Please take a few moments in silence to reflect on the passage, then share a word or phrase that has struck you (don't go into any depth). Pause to think about what others have said then after a second reading of the passage you can share a little more.

Reflection

In the Gospel passage to which we have just listened, the angel Gabriel greets Mary in a distinctive way. 'Rejoice, so highly favoured!' he says, 'The Lord is with you.' Commenting on the angel's greeting St. Thomas Aquinas highlights the uniqueness of this event, reminding us it was usually humans who made deference to angels, not angels to humanity. Here, however, a young teenage girl from Nazareth is reverently greeted by the angel Gabriel. Not even Abraham, the great father of the Israelites, was treated in this way (Genesis 18:1-15). In simple terms, there is no one like her, before or since – highly favoured, yet humble and faithful – chosen by God to bear the Saviour of all into the world.

While St. Paul, who was so fundamental in the spread of the early Church, is held up – rightly – as a model for Christian living and witness (1 Corinthians 11:1) some Christian traditions have difficulty in talking about Mary in a similar way. They can struggle with the emphasis which others such as the Catholics and Orthodox

Hail Mary
Full of Grace

place on Our Lady. Indeed, conscious of the way in which other Christian traditions approach Our Lady, she can seem something of an embarrassment – an obstacle to the unity her Son prayed for. Surely though, there is a place for both the unceasing action and energetic movement of Paul, and the quiet contemplation, pondering and simple presence of Our Lady.

Mary, the 'Theotokos' ('the one who gave birth to the one who is God'), was among the last at the foot of the Cross and one of the first in the Upper Room. She initiated Christ's ministry at Cana. With John the Baptist she was there at the crossroads of the Old and New Testaments; with the Apostles she was there at the birth of the Church. Where Peter fled, she remained; where Joseph feared, she feared not. For her fidelity, presence and courage she is due the honour she receives.

What memories of Marian devotions do you have? How does Mary feature in your prayer life? How would you describe your approach to Mary? We speak of Mary as Mother of God, Mother of the Church and Mother of us all. How do you understand these titles?

Closing Prayers
You may wish to end this session with one of the anthems or canticles on the inside cover of the book or you may wish to use some different prayers from pp.33-47 or 54-57.

Father, source of light in every age,
the Virgin conceived and bore your Son
who is called Wonderful God, Prince of Peace.
May her prayer, the gift of a mother's love,

Mary in the Scriptures (from *Lumen Gentium, 55*)
The Sacred Scriptures, as well as ancient Tradition show the role of the Mother of the Saviour in the economy of salvation... The books of the Old Testament describe the history of salvation, by which the coming of Christ was slowly prepared... bring[ing] the figure of the woman, Mother of the Redeemer, into a gradually clearer light. She is prophetically foreshadowed in the promise of victory over the serpent... Likewise she is the Virgin who shall conceive and bear a son, whose name will be called Emmanuel. She stands out among the poor and humble of the Lord, who confidently hope for and receive salvation from Him. With her, the exalted Daughter of Sion, the times are fulfilled and the new Economy established, when the Son of God took a human nature from her, that He might in the mysteries of His flesh free man from sin.

Hail Mary
Full of Grace

be your people's joy through all ages.
May her response, born of a humble heart,
draw your Spirit to rest on your people.
Grant this through Christ our Lord.
Amen.

Alternative Opening Prayer – Solemnity of Mary, Mother of God

Notes

Did you know... that the Qur'an (the Holy book of Islam) contains more references to Mary, Mother of Jesus, than the whole of the New Testament?

Immaculately conceived and assumed into heaven

That Mary was conceived without the stain of original sin was a long held belief which became dogma in 1854. While this may suggest that she was not in need of Christ's saving sacrifice, Blessed John Duns Scotus helps us to understand that as the Son of God exists outside of time his love and mediation redeemed her even before her birth ('preventive redemption'). Her sinless nature and sinless life, participating in the holiness of God, led her to be taken body and soul into heaven at the end of her time on earth.

Full of grace

Opening Prayers

Taken from the third poem of the Song of Songs 4:1-16

Leader: How beautiful you are, my love, how very beautiful!
Your eyes are doves behind your veil.
Your hair is like a flock of goats, moving down the slopes of Gilead.
Your lips are like a crimson thread, and your mouth is lovely.

Group: Until the day breathes and the shadows flee,
I will hasten to the mountain of myrrh and the hill of frankincense.

Leader: You are altogether beautiful, my love; there is no flaw in you.
You have ravished my heart, my sister, my bride,
you have ravished my heart with a glance of your eyes,
with one jewel of your necklace.

Group: Awake, O north wind, and come, O south wind!
Blow upon my garden that its fragrance may be wafted abroad.
Let my beloved come to his garden, and eat its choicest fruits.

All: Glory be to the Father, and to the Son and to the Holy Spirit. As it was in
the beginning, is now, and ever shall be, world without end. Amen.

*For a few moments, either aloud or in the silence of our hearts, let us give thanks to
the Lord for all the blessings we have received over the past week. As we give thanks
let us remember, again in silence or aloud, all those who need our prayers. The word
repent means to turn around - keeping in mind God's mercy, let us remember all the
times that we have turned from him and ask for his forgiveness.*

Introduction to Reading of Scripture

St. Matthew wrote: 'Ask and it will be given to you; search, and you will find; knock
and the door will be opened for you.' Let us now, with trust in the Father, seek
his will in reading, find it in meditating; knock in mental prayer for an opening to
God's love and wisdom through sharing and contemplation.

After Matthew 7:7 and Guido the Carthusian

Hail Mary
Full of Grace

Explore the Scriptures Genesis 3:1-13, 20-23

Now the serpent was craftier than any other wild animal that the Lord God had made. He said to the woman, 'Did God say, "You shall not eat from any tree in the garden"?' The woman said to the serpent, 'We may eat of the fruit of the trees in the garden; but God said, "You shall not eat of the fruit of the tree that is in the middle of the garden, nor shall you touch it, or you shall die."' But the serpent said to the woman, 'You will not die; for God knows that when you eat of it your eyes will be opened, and you will be like God, knowing good and evil.' So when the woman saw that the tree was good for food, and that it was a delight to the eyes, and that the tree was to be desired to make one wise, she took of its fruit and ate; and she also gave some to her husband, who was with her, and he ate. Then the eyes of both were opened, and they knew that they were naked; and they sewed fig leaves together and made loincloths for themselves.

They heard the sound of the Lord God walking in the garden at the time of the evening breeze, and the man and his wife hid themselves from the presence of the Lord God among the trees of the garden. But the Lord God called to the man, and said to him, 'Where are you?' He said, 'I heard the sound of you in the garden, and I was afraid, because I was naked; and I hid myself.' He said, 'Who told you that you were naked? Have you eaten from the tree of which I commanded you not to eat?' The man said, 'The woman whom you gave to be with me, she gave me fruit from the tree, and I ate.' Then the Lord God said to the woman, 'What is this that you have done?' The woman said, 'The serpent tricked me, and I ate.'

The man named his wife Eve, because she was the mother of all who live. And the Lord God made garments of skins for the man and for his wife, and clothed them. Then the Lord God said, 'See, the man has become like one of us, knowing good and evil; and now, he might reach out his hand and take also from the tree of life, and eat, and live for ever' – therefore the Lord God sent him forth from the garden of Eden, to till the ground from which he was taken.

Please take a few moments in silence to reflect on the passage, then share a word or

Mary's early years
Among the traditions that grew up around Mary – that her parents were called Joachim and Ann, that she was dedicated to the Temple as a child, that she gave birth to Jesus in a cave and that Joseph was elderly when Christ was born – come not from the canonical books we read in the Bible (Matthew, Mark, Luke and John), but from apocryphal documents, often fantastic and wildly embellished, such as the *Protoevangelium of James*, written to satisfy curiosity in the lives of the Holy Family in the early years after Our Lord's death.

Hail Mary
Full of Grace

phrase that has struck you (don't go into any depth). Pause to think about what others have said then after a second reading of the passage you can share a little more.

Reflection

Scripture gives us several stories of surprising pregnancies: Sarah, the wife of Abraham, conceived Isaac in her nineties (Genesis 21:1-7), despite being barren Manoah's wife conceived Samson (Judges 13:1-25) and Elizabeth – Mary's elderly cousin - conceived John the Baptist (Luke 1:7, 57-58). In one sense therefore Jesus' mother Mary was not alone, yet if hers is not the only miraculous pregnancy to be found in Scripture, she is unique in that she remained a virgin, conceiving by the power of the Holy Spirit.

Similarly, Mary was not the first woman to be created free from original sin. God of his very nature cannot do things badly. All that he does, he does perfectly. In the second story of creation we read in Genesis, when God created Adam and Eve, he creates them perfectly, without any spot, stain or blemish. Indeed we are told that he looked on what he had created and found it very good. This point is taken up by the Church Fathers, those early theologians and bishops, who were keen to point out that Eve, like Mary, was created perfectly and sinless. Yet if Eve and Mary have something quite fundamental in common, Mary is unique in that she remained sinless. For the whole of her life, and in all that she did, Mary remained open to God, freely choosing to do God's will. It is her continuous openness to God's action, God's grace, that led Mary to say 'yes' to being the mother of his Son and which distinguishes her from Eve. If, as St. Irenaeus writes, Eve played a part in the fall, so Mary, by her openness to grace, played a part in our redemption: 'what the virgin Eve had bound fast through unbelief, this did the Virgin Mary set free through faith.'

The Feast of the Immaculate Conception (8 December)

The Western Christian Church first celebrated a feast of the Conception of the Most Holy and All Pure Mother of God perhaps as early as the 5th century in Syria. By the 7th century it was a widely known feast in the East. In the same century the doctrine of Mary's spotlessness was included in the Qur'an. In 1854, Pius IX made the infallible statement *Ineffabilis Deus*: 'The most Blessed Virgin Mary, in the first instant of her conception, by a singular grace and privilege granted by almighty God, in view of the merits of Jesus Christ, the saviour of the human race, was preserved free from all stain of original sin.'

Gospel reading: Luke 1:26-38; **Morning Prayer**: Isaiah 43:1; **Midday Prayer**: Ephesians 1:11-12; **Evening Prayer**: Romans 5:20-21

Hail Mary
Full of Grace

Just as Christ is often referred to as the new or second Adam – the one who leads us to not away from eternal life – Mary is also referred to as the new or second Eve. In Mary we see freedom and real love coincide. Her acceptance of God's plan, opens up the life of grace for every one of us. In obedience to God's will, she conceived and gave birth, raised and then witnessed the death and resurrection of the one who 'brings everyone to life and makes them justified' (Romans 5:12-18).

Mary differed from Eve in that she exercised her free will in a very different way. How, over the past few weeks, have you succumbed to temptation? What stops you letting God in? Where, in your life, have you felt enlightened by God's presence?

Closing Prayers
You may wish to end this session with one of the anthems or canticles on the inside cover of the book or you may wish to use some different prayers from pp.33-47 or 54-57.

Father, source of light in every age,
the Virgin conceived and bore your Son
who is called Wonderful God, Prince of Peace.
May her prayer, the gift of a mother's love,
be your people's joy through all ages.
May her response, born of a humble heart,
draw your Spirit to rest on your people.
Grant this through Christ our Lord.
Amen.

Alternative Opening Prayer – Solemnity of Mary, Mother of God

 Notes

The Virgin Hodegetria (14th Century)

Hail Mary
Full of Grace

The Lord is with thee

Opening prayer
Taken from the book of Job 36:5-16

Leader: Surely God is mighty and does not despise any;
he is mighty in strength of understanding.
He does not keep the wicked alive, but gives the afflicted their right.

Group: He does not withdraw his eyes from the righteous,
but with kings on the throne he sets them for ever, and they are exalted.
And if they are bound in fetters and caught in the cords of affliction,
then he declares to them their work
and their transgressions, that they are behaving arrogantly.

Leader: He opens their ears to instruction, and commands that they return from
iniquity.
If they listen, and serve him, they complete their days in prosperity,
and their years in pleasantness.
But if they do not listen, they shall perish by the sword,
and die without knowledge.

Group: The godless in heart cherish anger;
they do not cry for help when he binds them.
They die in their youth, and their life ends in shame.
He delivers the afflicted by their affliction, and opens their ear by adversity.

Leader: For you, no less, he plans relief from sorrow.

All: Glory be to the Father, and to the Son and to the Holy Spirit. As it was in
the beginning, is now, and ever shall be, world without end. Amen.

*For a few moments, either aloud or in the silence of our hearts, let us give thanks to
the Lord for all the blessings we have received over the past week. As we give thanks
let us remember, again in silence or aloud, all those who need our prayers. The word
repent means to turn around - keeping in mind God's mercy, let us remember all the
times that we have turned from him and ask for his forgiveness.*

Hail Mary
Full of Grace

Introduction to Reading of Scripture

St. Matthew wrote: 'Ask and it will be given to you; search, and you will find; knock and the door will be opened for you.' Let us now, with trust in the Father, seek his will in reading, find it in meditating; knock in mental prayer for an opening to God's love and wisdom through sharing and contemplation.

After Matthew 7:7 and Guido the Carthusian

Explore the Scriptures John 19:16-30

So they took Jesus; and carrying the cross by himself, he went out to what is called The Place of the Skull, which in Hebrew is called Golgotha. There they crucified him, and with him two others, one on either side, with Jesus between them. Pilate also had an inscription written and put on the cross. It read, 'Jesus of Nazareth, the King of the Jews.' Many of the Jews read this inscription, because the place where Jesus was crucified was near the city; and it was written in Hebrew, in Latin, and in Greek. Then the chief priests of the Jews said to Pilate, 'Do not write, "The King of the Jews", but, "This man said, I am King of the Jews."' Pilate answered, 'What I have written I have written.' When the soldiers had crucified Jesus, they took his clothes and divided them into four parts, one for each soldier. They also took his tunic; now the tunic was seamless, woven in one piece from the top. So they said to one another, 'Let us not tear it, but cast lots for it to see who will get it.' This was to fulfil what the scripture says:

'They divided my clothes among themselves, and for my clothing they cast lots.'

And that is what the soldiers did. Meanwhile, standing near the cross of Jesus were his mother, and his mother's sister, Mary the wife of Clopas, and Mary Magdalene. When Jesus saw his mother and the disciple whom he loved standing beside her, he said to his mother, 'Woman, here is your son.' Then he said to the disciple, 'Here is your mother.' And from that hour the disciple took her into his own home.

After this, when Jesus knew that all was now finished, he said (in order to fulfil the scripture), 'I am thirsty.' A jar full of sour wine was standing there. So they put a sponge full of the wine on a branch of hyssop and held it to his mouth. When Jesus had received the wine, he said, 'It is finished.' Then he bowed his head and gave up his spirit.

Reflection

When we pray the *Hail Mary* we assert that the Lord is with Mary, 'the Lord is with thee'. For us, however, when faced with the toil of daily living, let alone the challenge of serious tragedy, the Lord can seem a million miles away. With the

Hail Mary
Full of Grace

prophet Job, we can cry out, asking the Lord where he has gone and why he has deserted us. However, Mary's life was not without its difficulties, yet still we speak of the Lord being with her.

Breaking the news of her pregnancy what judgements and prejudices must Mary have encountered? How did she face fiancé, family and friends? As she followed the dusty trail from Nazareth to Bethlehem she must have wondered what the angel's promise would mean for her child, for Joseph, for her. In Bethlehem itself she knew what it felt like to be homeless, pregnant and unable to find a place to give birth. And then, once Jesus had been born, she experienced the fear and uncertainty of being on the run and in danger – fleeing to Egypt to avoid the persecution of Herod.

If Mary had the 'luxury' of knowing something of her Son's future: 'He will be great and will be called Son of the Most High' (Luke 1:32), she also knew, as Simeon had warned, that her boy was 'destined to be a sign that is rejected' (Luke 2:34). No doubt the neighbours would have heard and shared the news of what Jesus got up to, his sitting down with sinners as much as his healing of the sick. And then, for all the triumph of his entry into Jerusalem, for all his being hailed as 'King of the Jews', Mary's was a ringside view of his cruel and painful death, a tragedy made all the worse by the desertion of his followers.

Faced with suffering we can think of ourselves as being unfortunate or hard done by. Curiously though, we can encounter and be challenged by those who have suffered much, sacrificed a lot and yet remain cheerful and upbeat. In Scripture, as the Beatitudes show (Matthew 5:1-12), suffering is often presented as a blessing. Blessed or happy are those who are persecuted, happy are those who mourn and suffer abuse.

Our Lady of Sorrows (15 September)

From the prophecy of Simeon and the flight to Egypt to the sorrow at the foot of the Cross, Mary suffered for and with her beloved Son and Saviour. Her sufferings are frequently recalled at this memorial by the recitation of the *Stabat Mater Dolorosa* ('the sorrowful mother stood' - a sequence attributed to Innocent III and often used during the Stations of the Cross).

The Seven Sorrows of Mary are listed as: *the Prophecy of Simeon, the Flight into Egypt, the Loss of Jesus in the temple, the Meeting of Jesus and Mary on the Way of the Cross, the Crucifixion, the Taking Down of the Body of Jesus from the Cross, and Jesus laid in the Tomb.*

Hail Mary
Full of Grace

Like Christ, suffering and pain also characterised the lives of his disciples chief among whom was Mary. It is easy to place Mary's life on a pedestal and, in highlighting the ways in which she was blessed, to forget the pain and difficulties which her being blessed involved. Being close to God, being close to Jesus, does not guarantee us a life free of suffering or pain. In both joy and in sorrow we, like Mary, are challenged to lives of loving and full-hearted giving; lives which proclaim the joy and hope we have in the Lord. Mary saw, and we know, that the suffering of her Son was not the end. Her little manger-born boy, our Christ, triumphed over death and sin to become 'a light to enlighten the pagans and the glory of Israel' (Luke 2:32).

Mary, though blessed and loved by God, suffered pain and prejudice. Where have you felt close to God in suffering? What sacrifices have you made for your faith?

Closing Prayers
You may wish to end this session with one of the anthems or canticles on the inside cover of the book or you may wish to use some different prayers from pp.33-47 or 54-57.

Father, source of light in every age,
the Virgin conceived and bore your Son
who is called Wonderful God, Prince of Peace.
May her prayer, the gift of a mother's love,
be your people's joy through all ages.
May her response, born of a humble heart,
draw your Spirit to rest on your people.
Grant this through Christ our Lord.
Amen.

Alternative Opening Prayer – Solemnity of Mary, Mother of God

 Notes

Full of Grace

Pieta (after Eugène Delacroix) by Vincent van Gogh (1889)

Hail Mary
Full of Grace

Blessed art thou among women

Opening prayer

The Song of Hannah which can be found in the first book of Samuel 2:1-10

Leader: Hannah prayed and said:
'My heart exults in the Lord;
my strength is exalted in my God.
My mouth derides my enemies, because I rejoice in my victory.

Group: 'There is no Holy One like the Lord, no one besides you;
there is no Rock like our God.
Talk no more so very proudly,
let not arrogance come from your mouth;
for the Lord is a God of knowledge, and by him actions are weighed.

Leader: 'The bows of the mighty are broken, but the feeble gird on strength.
Those who were full have hired themselves out for bread,
but those who were hungry are fat with spoil.
The barren has borne seven, but she who has many children is forlorn.

Group: 'The Lord kills and brings to life;
he brings down to Sheol and raises up.
The Lord makes poor and makes rich; he brings low, he also exalts.
He raises up the poor from the dust;
he lifts the needy from the ash heap,
to make them sit with princes and inherit a seat of honour.
For the pillars of the earth are the Lord's, and on them he has set the world.

Leader: 'He will guard the feet of his faithful ones,
but the wicked shall be cut off in darkness; for not by might does one prevail.
The Lord! His adversaries shall be shattered;
the Most High will thunder in heaven.
The Lord will judge the ends of the earth;
he will give strength to his king, and exalt the power of his anointed.'

All: Glory be to the Father, and to the Son and to the Holy Spirit. As it was in
the beginning, is now, and ever shall be, world without end. Amen.

Hail Mary
Full of Grace

For a few moments, either aloud or in the silence of our hearts, let us give thanks to the Lord for all the blessings we have received over the past week. As we give thanks let us remember, again in silence or aloud, all those who need our prayers. The word repent means to turn around - keeping in mind God's mercy, let us remember all the times that we have turned from him and ask for his forgiveness.

Introduction to Reading of Scripture

St. Matthew wrote: 'Ask and it will be given to you; search, and you will find; knock and the door will be opened for you.' Let us now, with trust in the Father, seek his will in reading, find it in meditating; knock in mental prayer for an opening to God's love and wisdom through sharing and contemplation.

After Matthew 7:7 and Guido the Carthusian

Explore the Scriptures Luke 1:39-56

In those days Mary set out and went with haste to a Judean town in the hill country, where she entered the house of Zechariah and greeted Elizabeth. When Elizabeth heard Mary's greeting, the child leapt in her womb. And Elizabeth was filled with the Holy Spirit and exclaimed with a loud cry, 'Blessed are you among women, and blessed is the fruit of your womb. And why has this happened to me, that the mother of my Lord comes to me? For as soon as I heard the sound of your greeting, the child in my womb leapt for joy. And blessed is she who believed that there would be a fulfilment of what was spoken to her by the Lord.'

And Mary said:

'My soul magnifies the Lord, and my spirit rejoices in God my Saviour, for he has looked with favour on the lowliness of his servant. Surely, from now on all generations will call me blessed; for the Mighty One has done great things for me, and holy is his name. His mercy is for those who fear him from generation to generation. He has shown strength with his arm; he has scattered the proud in the thoughts of their hearts. He has brought down the powerful from their thrones, and lifted up the lowly; he has filled the hungry with good things, and sent the rich away empty. He has helped his servant Israel, in remembrance of his mercy, according to the promise he made to our ancestors, to Abraham and to his descendants for ever.'

And Mary remained with her for about three months and then returned to her home.

Please take a few moments in silence to reflect on the passage, then share a word or phrase that has struck you (don't go into any depth). Pause to think about what others have said then after a second reading of the passage you can share a little more.

Hail Mary
Full of Grace

Reflection

Mary was blessed in a number of ways; blessed because she was not marked by sin, blessed because she was taken up into heaven at the end of her life on earth, blessed because she was given the privilege of being the mother of Christ. We have already reflected on Mary's openness to God's plan, an openness that allowed his grace, his action, to take root and live in her, but today's passage brings out another aspect of Mary's blessedness. Setting out into the hill country, to Ein Karim in Judah, Mary goes to visit her aging cousin, Elizabeth. Stirred by the Holy Spirit, Elizabeth proclaims Mary as 'blessed' – blessed because she was to be the mother of the Lord and blessed because she had trusted in what the angel had said to her.

Few would doubt the importance of asking questions and testing the 'facts', the reliability or truth of what is said to us about someone or something. Indeed, the honing of our critical faculties and our powers of discernment is a crucial part of what it is to make mature decisions. Nonetheless, we tend to take a lot of things on trust. We trust that the consultant, architect, and electrician know what they are doing. We trust that the chef has no desire to poison us, that the car manufacturer wants the car to work and that the taxi driver and pilot have every intention of arriving safely. Inevitably there will be times when our trust will seem misplaced; when things do not go according to plan and the reputable brand or the best friend lets us down. Here, it would be easy for cynicism to take hold; to question as a matter of course, the worth and value of almost everything, friendship included.

Mary's trusting is an antidote to such cynicism. In trusting what the angel had to say, she abandoned herself to God's will, surrendering whatever plans she may have had for her own future. In Mary we are reminded of the close connection between trust and faith. Faith, as Mary demonstrates, takes a lot of things on trust,

The Patronage of the Blessed Virgin Mary

In times of trouble we turn to God with the prayers of Mary and the saints. Different professions and countries, individual parishes, even families have and invoke their own patrons. The Blessed Virgin Mary is cited as the patroness of all humanity. However, certain occupations and activities are more closely associated with her protection:

airplane crews and pilots, bicyclists, blood donors, Carmelites, Cistercians, clothworkers, coffee-house keepers, construction workers, cooks, fishermen, gold and silversmiths, Jesuits, mothers, nuns, potters, restauranteurs, ribbonmakers, sailors, tilemakers, upholsterers, army personnel, virgins and yachtsmen to name but a few!

Hail Mary
Full of Grace

a trust which the believer would see as wholly reasonable, but which society in general finds difficult to grasp. Where the ability to trust is undermined, where the natural reaction is to see the worst, instead of seeing the best, the seedbed of faith – the hope within us - is undermined.

Throughout his ministry Jesus continued to see the best in others, refusing to let the knowledge of their faults and failings colour his appreciation of all that they could be. In striving to live as Christ lived let us call on the prayers of Mary that in imitating her trust we might hear anew Christ's own words to us: 'Blessed are those who have not seen and yet have come to believe (John 20:29).

What did you take on trust as a child? What do you take on trust today? What part does trust play in your faith? What do you think you can learn from Mary?

Closing Prayers
You may wish to end this session with one of the anthems or canticles on the inside cover of the book or you may wish to use some different prayers from pp.33-47 or 54-57.

Father, source of light in every age,
the Virgin conceived and bore your Son
who is called Wonderful God, Prince of Peace.
May her prayer, the gift of a mother's love,
be your people's joy through all ages.
May her response, born of a humble heart,
draw your Spirit to rest on your people.
Grant this through Christ our Lord.
Amen.

Alternative Opening Prayer – Solemnity of Mary, Mother of God

---

 Notes

Did you know... that the *Stabat Mater* has been set to music by many composers including Palestrina, Haydn and Verdi and was on Dutch rock band Epica's first album?

Hail Mary
Full of Grace

Blessed is the fruit of thy womb, Jesus

session five

Opening prayer

The Divine Praises: originally written by Luigi Felici, S.J. in 1797 to make reparations against blasphemy and profanity were expanded upon by Pope Pius VII in 1801.

Read together slowly

Blessed be God.
Blessed be His Holy Name.
Blessed be Jesus Christ, true God and true man.
Blessed be the name of Jesus.
Blessed be His Most Sacred Heart.
Blessed be Jesus in the Most Holy Sacrament of the Altar.
Blessed be the Holy Spirit, the Paraclete.
Blessed be the great Mother of God, Mary most holy.
Blessed be her holy and Immaculate Conception.
Blessed be her glorious Assumption.
Blessed be the name of Mary, Virgin and Mother.
Blessed be Saint Joseph, her most chaste spouse.
Blessed be God in His angels and in His Saints.
Amen.

For a few moments, either aloud or in the silence of our hearts, let us give thanks to the Lord for all the blessings we have received over the past week. As we give thanks let us remember, again in silence or aloud, all those who need our prayers. The word repent means to turn around - keeping in mind God's mercy, let us remember all the times that we have turned from him and ask for his forgiveness.

Introduction to Reading of Scripture

St. Matthew wrote: 'Ask and it will be given to you; search, and you will find; knock and the door will be opened for you.' Let us now, with trust in the Father, seek his will in reading, find it in meditating; knock in mental prayer for an opening to God's love and wisdom through sharing and contemplation.

After Matthew 7:7 and Guido the Carthusian

Hail Mary
Full of Grace

Explore the Scriptures Apocalypse 11:19; 12:1-6, 10-11
This is the first Reading from Day Mass of the Assumption of the Blessed Virgin Mary

Then God's temple in heaven was opened, and the ark of his covenant was seen within his temple; and there were flashes of lightning, rumblings, peals of thunder, an earthquake, and heavy hail.

A great portent appeared in heaven: a woman clothed with the sun, with the moon under her feet, and on her head a crown of twelve stars. She was pregnant and was crying out in birth pangs, in the agony of giving birth. Then another portent appeared in heaven: a great red dragon, with seven heads and ten horns, and seven diadems on his heads. His tail swept down a third of the stars of heaven and threw them to the earth. Then the dragon stood before the woman who was about to bear a child, so that he might devour her child as soon as it was born. And she gave birth to a son, a male child, who is to rule all the nations with a rod of iron. But her child was snatched away and taken to God and to his throne; and the woman fled into the wilderness, where she has a place prepared by God.

Then I heard a loud voice in heaven, proclaiming, 'Now have come the salvation and the power and the kingdom of our God and the authority of his Messiah, for the accuser of our comrades has been thrown down, who accuses them day and night before our God. But they have conquered him by the blood of the Lamb and by the word of their testimony, for they did not cling to life even in the face of death.'

Please take a few moments in silence to reflect on the passage, then share a word or phrase that has struck you (don't go into any depth). Pause to think about what others have said then after a second reading of the passage you can share a little more.

Reflection
Over the centuries the Litany of Our Lady of Loreto has been recited by millions of people. This litany attributes to Mary a number of titles. Some of these are

The Childhood
of Jesus
Westminster
Cathedral mosaic

Hail Mary
Full of Grace

scriptural. Some of them traditional. The titles can be grouped into four sections: Mary as Mother (of Christ, of the Church, most pure), Mary as Virgin (most renowned, most faithful), Mary as Queen (of all saints, of the Family, of peace) and some wonderful descriptions such as Gate of Heaven, Mystical Rose, Morning Star, Cause of our Joy and Ark of the Covenant.

The Ark of the Covenant was a gilded box built to contain the tablets on which the Ten Commandments were inscribed, manna (bread) and the rod of Aaron symbolising priesthood (Hebrews 9:4). In today's Scripture passage, having seen the Ark, the writer of the book of the Apocalypse describes the birthpangs of a women giving birth to a son, a male child, who is to rule all the nations. Mary is the New Ark, bearing forth not manna but the Bread of Life, not the rod of Aaron but the eternal high priest, not the word on stone but the Word in flesh, Jesus Christ.

This 'Jesus Christ' is the fruit of Mary's womb. He is the Son of God who rewrites the relationship between us and the Father in his own blood. He is the perfect sacrifice acceptable to God, whose life, death and resurrection has thrown open, once and for all, the floodgates of forgiveness. Each time we celebrate the Eucharist Christ's self-sacrifice, his rewriting of the covenant between us and God is re-presented to us. Indeed, when we receive Christ's Body and Blood we, like Mary, are one with Christ. In this way we are afforded the privilege of bearing the Lord and of being, like her, 'arks of the covenant'. When Mary discovered the Christ-child alive in her, she did not keep this to herself but she rushed to see her kinswoman Elizabeth in order to share the Good News (Luke 1:39). The challenge

The Blessed Virgin Mary and Advent

The Liturgy celebrates the BVM in an exemplary way during the season of Advent. It recalls the women of the Old Testament who prefigured and prophesied her mission; it exalts her faith and the humility with which she promptly and totally submitted to God's plan of salvation; it highlights her presence in the events of grace preceding the birth of the Saviour. Popular piety also devotes particular attention to the BVM during Advent, as is evident from the many pious exercises practised at this time, especially the novena of the Immaculate Conception and of Christmas.

In the Oriental Churches, Advent is Marian in character while highlighting that all Marian mysteries refer to the mystery of our salvation in Christ. In the Coptic rite, the Lauds of the BVM are sung in the *Theotokia*. Among the Syrians, Advent is referred to as the *Subbara* or Annunciation. The Byzantine Rite prepares for Christmas with a whole series of Marian feasts and rituals.

Hail Mary
Full of Grace

of every Eucharist is remembering it as the touchstone of our life of faith and of our mission, the sharing with others the fruit we have received.

We are told in the Scriptures that Mary pondered the things she was told. They were not taken for granted. Is the privilege of receiving the Lord in communion, allowing us to be 'arks of the covenant' something which you take for granted? Do you use the silence after communion to reflect on what you have received? How can you, like Mary, cherish the Word and bear his life, message and love to those around you?

Closing Prayers

You may wish to end this session with one of the anthems or canticles on the inside cover of the book or you may wish to use some different prayers from pp.33-47 or 54-57.

Father, source of light in every age,
the Virgin conceived and bore your Son
who is called Wonderful God, Prince of Peace.
May her prayer, the gift of a mother's love,
be your people's joy through all ages.
May her response, born of a humble heart,
draw your Spirit to rest on your people.
Grant this through Christ our Lord.
Amen.

Alternative Opening Prayer – Solemnity of Mary, Mother of God

 Notes

Holy Mary, Mother of God, pray for us

Opening prayer

Taken from Psalm 77(78) 15-18, 23-24, 32-33, 38, 72

Leader: He split the rocks in the desert.
He gave them plentiful drink as from the deep.
He made streams flow out from the rock
and made waters run down like rivers.

Group: Yet still they sinned against him;
they defied the Most High in the desert.
In their heart they put God to the test
by demanding the food they craved.

Leader: Yet he commanded the clouds above
and opened the gates of heaven.
He rained down manna for their food,
and gave them bread from heaven.

Group: Despite this they went on sinning;
they had no faith in his wonders:
so he ended their days like a breath
and their years in sudden ruin.

Leader: Yet he who is full of compassion
forgave them their sin and spared them.
So often he held back his anger
when he might have stirred up his rage.
He tended them with blameless heart,
with discerning mind he led them.

All: Glory be to the Father, and to the Son and to the Holy Spirit. As it was in the beginning, is now, and ever shall be, world without end. Amen.

For a few moments, either aloud or in the silence of our hearts, let us give thanks to the Lord for all the blessings we have received over the past week. As we give thanks let us remember, again in silence or aloud, all those who need our prayers. The word repent means to turn around - keeping in mind God's mercy, let us remember all the times that we have turned from him and ask for his forgiveness.

Hail Mary
Full of Grace

Introduction to Reading of Scripture

St. Matthew wrote: 'Ask and it will be given to you; search, and you will find; knock and the door will be opened for you.' Let us now, with trust in the Father, seek his will in reading, find it in meditating; knock in mental prayer for an opening to God's love and wisdom through sharing and contemplation.

After Matthew 7:7 and Guido the Carthusian

Explore the Scriptures John 2:1-12

This reading is heard on the 7th January if before the Epiphany and on the 2nd Sunday of Ordinary Time (Year C)

On the third day there was a wedding in Cana of Galilee, and the mother of Jesus was there. Jesus and his disciples had also been invited to the wedding. When the wine gave out, the mother of Jesus said to him, 'They have no wine.' And Jesus said to her, 'Woman, what concern is that to you and to me? My hour has not yet come.' His mother said to the servants, 'Do whatever he tells you.' Now standing there were six stone water-jars for the Jewish rites of purification, each holding twenty or thirty gallons. Jesus said to them, 'Fill the jars with water.' And they filled them up to the brim. He said to them, 'Now draw some out, and take it to the chief steward.' So they took it. When the steward tasted the water that had become wine, and did not know where it came from (though the servants who had drawn the water knew), the steward called the bridegroom and said to him, 'Everyone serves the good wine first, and then the inferior wine after the guests have become drunk. But you have kept the good wine until now.' Jesus did this, the first of his signs, in Cana of Galilee, and revealed his glory; and his disciples believed in him. After this he went down to Capernaum with his mother, his brothers, and his disciples; and they remained there for a few days.

Please take a few moments in silence to reflect on the passage, then share a word or phrase that has struck you (don't go into any depth). Pause to think about what others have said then after a second reading of the passage you can share a little more.

St Joseph

Not much is known of Joseph, foster-father of Jesus. In works of art he is frequently portrayed as an old man (and refered to as a widower). In the mosaic image to the left he is, however, shown as a young man with his young bride. Matthew's gospel refers to him as 'tekton', Greek for an artisan working with wood or iron and Mark writes of him teaching his craft to Jesus. Joseph's care and provision for Mary and Jesus has led to him being named patron saint of the Universal Church, of fathers, of workers and of migrants.

Hail Mary
Full of Grace

Reflection

In the Acts of the Apostles, St. Peter proclaims Jesus, raised up by God, to be 'leader and saviour' (Acts 5:31). The Greek word used for leader in this instance is 'archegos,' which can be translated as 'path-breaker', one who points out the road to what is above and beyond. In today's gospel passage it is Mary who takes the initiative. She, in a sense, is the 'archegos' (or 'archegissa'!) who points us to Christ.

Mary could have rolled her eyes at the couple's lack of preparedness and observed their embarrassment from a distance. Instead she sets to work and pleads with her son, initiating his first miracle and the beginning of his public ministry. At Cana therefore Mary demonstrates her concern for the needs of others and shows her willingness to act on their behalf. It is part of our tradition that Mary will do for us today what she did for the couple at Cana, that now as then she seeks to share our burdens, to intercede on our behalf.

The Bible presents us with a much broader understanding of family or kinship than we have today. In fact, of the 350 references to 'brother' in the Bible, the vast majority have nothing to do with blood relationships (e.g. Tobit 5-6 and Acts 1:15-16). In Christ we are related, we are family, not because we share the same blood but because we have been baptised by the Spirit into Him. At the foot of the Cross, Jesus entrusts his disciple John to Mary as her son and entrusts Mary to John as his mother. The implication is clear. If we, as followers or disciples of Christ, see John as our brother we must also look on Mary as our mother.

As the mother of Christ and our mother, Mary is uniquely placed to pray for us. Indeed, at the end of her life, Tradition holds that Mary, who lived her life in complete communion with God, was taken up or assumed into heaven where

The Feast of the Assumption of the BVM (15 August)

Tradition teaches and it is an article of belief that Mary was taken (assumed) body and soul into heaven (CCC, 966). Just as the empty tomb helps us to believe in Christ's Resurrection, the Apostles returned to the Tomb of Mary (close to Mount Zion) and too found it empty. The Early Church thereafter celebrated the 'Memory of Mary' each year. Although it has these ancient roots it was not until 1950 that, in the Apostolic Constitution *Munificentissimus Deus*, Pope Pius XII proclaimed that the Assumption of Mary was a dogma of the Catholic Church. It is celebrated in the Christian East as the Dormition of the Blessed Virgin Mary.

Gospel reading: Luke 1:39-56; **Morning Prayer:** Isaiah 61:10; **Midday Prayer:** Revelation 12:1; **Evening Prayer:** 1 Cor 15:22-23

Hail Mary
Full of Grace

she pleads directly to our loving Father. The goal of our Christian pilgrimage is to follow her into the eternal life of God's Kingdom. The key to that Kingdom is to be found in Christ. 'He shows us the way, and this way is the truth,' Pope Benedict XVI writes, 'Jesus Christ himself is both the way and the truth, and therefore he is also the life which all of us are seeking' (*Spe Salvi*, 6). Mary is truly our mother in that she seeks always and everywhere – in her act of giving birth, at Cana in Galilee, and from her place in heaven – to put us in communion with Christ who is the answer to our need.

Mary saw a need and acted upon it telling the servants to do whatever Christ told them. When have you, faced with another's need, choosen to keep a distance, refusing to get involved? How would you, today, respond to the command 'do whatever he tells you'? Are there areas of your life where you find it had to positively respond to this command?

Closing Prayers
You may wish to end this session with one of the anthems or canticles on the inside cover of the book or you may wish to use some different prayers from pp.33-47 or 54-57.

Father, source of light in every age,
the Virgin conceived and bore your Son
who is called Wonderful God, Prince of Peace.
May her prayer, the gift of a mother's love,
be your people's joy through all ages.
May her response, born of a humble heart,
draw your Spirit to rest on your people.
Grant this through Christ our Lord.
Amen.

Alternative Opening Prayer – Solemnity of Mary, Mother of God

 Notes

The Assumption of the Virgin by Peter Paul Rubens (1612–17)

Hail Mary
Full of Grace

Daily Prayer
Sunday to Saturday

The daily prayers on the following pages are drawn from the Divine Office (Liturgy of the Hours). Each day contains a Scripture reading, a psalm or Old Testament canticle and a selection of prayers based around an event in the life of Mary.

Together with the Mass, the Divine Office (Liturgy of the Hours) constitutes the official public prayer life of the Church. It is celebrated, under different names, in both the Eastern and Western Churches.

'The Office is... the prayer not only of the clergy but of the whole People of God.'   *Apostolic Constitution, Canticum Laudis*

Hail Mary
Full of Grace

Sunday - Mother of God

Introduction

O God, come to our aid. Lord, make haste to help us.

Glory be to the Father and to the Son and to the Holy Spirit, as it was in the beginning, is now, and ever shall be, world without end. Amen. (Alleluia)

omit Alleluias during Lent

Hymn

Maiden, yet a mother,
Daughter of thy Son,
High beyond all other, Lowlier is none;
Thou the consummation
Planned by God's decree,
When our lost creation
Nobler rose in thee!

Thus His place prepared,
He Who all things made
'Mid His creatures tarried, in thy bosom laid;
There His love He nourished,
Warmth that gave increase
To the root whence flourished
Our eternal peace.

Nor alone thou hearest
When thy name we hail;
Often thou art nearest when our voices fail;
Mirrored in thy fashion all creation's good,
Mercy might, compassion
Grace thy womanhood.

Lady, lest our vision,
Striving heavenward, fail,
Still let thy petition with thy Son prevail,
Unto whom all merit,
Power and majesty,
With the Holy Spirit
And the Father be.

Dante Aligheri 1265-1321
Tr. R A Knox 1888-1957

Antiphon

O how wonderful exchange! The Creator of human nature took on a human body and was born of the Virgin. He became man without having a human father and has bestowed on us his divine nature.

Psalmody

Psalm 112(113)

Praise, O servants of the Lord,
praise the name of the Lord!
May the name of the Lord be blessed
both now and for evermore!
From the rising of the sun to its setting
praised be the name of the Lord!

High above all nations is the Lord,
above the heavens his glory.
Who is like the Lord, our God,
who has risen on high to his throne
yet stoops from the heights to look down,
to look down upon heaven and earth?

From the dust he lifts up the lowly,
from their misery he raises the poor
to set them in the company of princes,
yes, with the princes of his people.
To the childless wife he gives a home
and gladdens her heart with children.

Glory be…

Antiphon

O how wonderful exchange! The Creator of human nature took on a human body and was born of the Virgin. He became man without having a human father and has bestowed on us his divine nature.

Hail Mary
Full of Grace

Reading
Micah 5:3-5

Therefore only so long as a woman is in labour shall he give up Israel;
and then those that survive of his race shall rejoin their brethren.
He shall appear and be their shepherd in the strength of the Lord, in the majesty of the name of the Lord his God, and he shall be a man of peace.

Short Responsory

℟ The Lord has made known our salvation, alleluia, alleluia.
℣ He has revealed his saving power.
Glory be…

Antiphon

God loved us so much that he sent his own Son in a mortal nature like ours: he was born of a woman, he was born subject to the Law, alleluia.

Benedictus (if said in the morning) or Magnificat (if said in the evening) - see inside back cover for these prayers

Intercessions

Blessed be the Lord Jesus, our bond of peace with one another.
℟ Lord, give peace to all.
Lord Jesus you revealed the meaning of human living; may we never fail to give you thanks.
℟ Lord, give peace to all.
You made Mary, your Mother, full of grace; enrich the lives of all with your blessings.
℟ Lord, give peace to all.

Our Father…

Concluding prayer

God, our Father,
Since you gave mankind a saviour through blessed Mary,
Virgin and mother,
Grant that we may feel the power of her intercession
when she pleads for us with Jesus Christ, your Son,
the author of life,
Who lives and reigns with you and the Holy Spirit,
God, for ever and ever.
Amen.

Hail Mary
Full of Grace

Monday - Conceived immaculate

Introduction
O God, come to our aid. Lord, make haste to help us.

Glory be to the Father and to the Son and to the Holy Spirit, as it was in the beginning, is now, and ever shall be, world without end. Amen. Alleluia.

Hymn
Holy light on earth's horizon,
Star of hope to those who fall,
Light amid a world of shadows,
Dawn of God's design for all.
Chosen from eternal ages,
You alone of all our race,
By your Son's atoning merits
Were conceived in perfect grace.

Mother of the world's Redeemer,
Promised from the dawn of time;
How could one so highly favoured
Share the guilt of Adam's crime?
Sun and moon and star adorn you,
Sinless Eve, triumphant sign;
you it is who crushed the serpent,
Mary, pledge of life divine.

Earth below and highest heaven
Praise the splendour of your state,
You who now are crowned in glory
Were conceived immaculate.
Hail, beloved of the Father,
Mother of his only Son,
Mystic bride of Love eternal,
Hail, O fair and spotless one!

Antiphon
Blessed are you, O Virgin Mary, above all women on earth. The Lord God himself has chosen you.

Psalmody
Psalm 62 (63)
O God, you are my God, for you I long;
for you my soul is thirsting.
My body pines for you
like a dry, weary land without water.
So I gaze on you in the sanctuary
to see your strength and your glory.

For your love is better than life,
my lips will speak your praise.
So I will bless you all my life,
in your name I will lift up my hands.
My soul shall be filled as with a banquet,
my mouth shall praise you with joy.

On my bed I remember you.
On you I muse through the night
for your have been my help;
in the shadow of your wings I rejoice.
My soul clings to you;
your right hand holds me fast.

Glory be...

Antiphon
Blessed are you, O Virgin Mary, above all women on earth. The Lord God himself has chosen you.

Reading
Ephesians 5:25-27
Christ loved the Church and sacrificed himself for her to make her holy, so that when he took her to himself she would be glorious, with no speck or wrinkle or anything like that, but holy and faultless.

Hail Mary
Full of Grace

Short Responsory

℟ The Lord has made known our salvation, alleluia, alleluia.

℣ He has revealed his saving power.

Glory be…

Antiphon

Hail, Mary, full of grace: the Lord is with you. You are the most blessed of all women, and blessed is the fruit of your womb, alleluia.

Benedictus (if said in the morning) or Magnificat (if said in the evening) - see inside back cover for these prayers

Intercessions

Let us praise God the Father who chose Mary as the mother of his Son and wanted all generations to call her blessed.

℟ May the Virgin Mary intercede for us.

Father you did great things for the Virgin Mary; fill the hearts of your children with the hope of Christ's glory.

℟ May the Virgin Mary intercede for us.

Through the prayers of Mary, our mother, heal the sick, comfort the sorrowful, pardon sinners; grant peace and salvation to all.

℟ May the Virgin Mary intercede for us.

You exalted the Virgin Mary and crowned her queen of heaven; may the dead enter your kingdom and rejoice with the saints for ever.

℟ May the Virgin Mary intercede for us.

Our Father…

Concluding prayer

Father,
we rejoice in the privilege of our Lady's Immaculate Conception,
which preserved her from the stain of sin by the power of Christ's redeeming death, and prepared her to be the Mother of God.
Grant that through her prayers
we ourselves may come to you,
cleansed from all sin.
We make our prayer through Christ, our Lord.
Amen.

Hail Mary
Full of Grace

Tuesday - Annunciation

Introduction
O God, come to our aid. Lord, make haste to help us.

Glory be to the Father and to the Son and to the Holy Spirit, as it was in the beginning, is now, and ever shall be, world without end. Amen. Alleluia.

Hymn
All creation was renewed
By the power of God most high,
When his promise was fulfilled
Adam's sons to justify.

By the Holy Spirit's love,
God pronounced his saving Word,
Then, with free consent and trust,
Mary bore creation's Lord.

Moment of unequalled faith,
Here in any time or place –
Thus did God put on our flesh
In his Virgin, full of grace.

Christ, the holy One of God,
Son of David, Light from Light,
Dwells with men, his glory dimmed
Till he comes again with might.

Father, Son and Spirit praise
For this marvel they have done;
In this act of perfect love,
Undivided, always One.

Antiphon
The angel Gabriel was sent to the Virgin Mary who was betrothed to Joseph.

Psalmody

Psalm 149

Sing a new song to the Lord,
his praise in the assembly of the faithful.
Let Israel rejoice in its Maker,
let Zion's sons exult in their king.
Let them praise his name with dancing
and make music with timbrel and harp.

For the Lord takes delight in his people.
He crowns the poor with salvation.
Let the faithful rejoice in their glory,
shout for joy and take their rest.
Let the praise of God be on their lips
and a two-edged sword in their hand,

to deal out vengeance to the nations
and punishment on all the peoples;
to bind their kings in chains
and their nobles in fetters of iron;
to carry out the sentence pre-ordained:
this honour is for all his faithful. Alleluia!

Glory be...

Antiphon
The angel Gabriel was sent to the Virgin Mary who was betrothed to Joseph.

Reading

1 John 4:10

This is what love is: it is not that we have loved God, but that he loved us and sent his Son to be the means by which our sins are forgiven.

Short Responsory
℟ A shoot has sprung from the stock of Jesse; a star has risen from Jacob.
℣ The Virgin has given birth to the Saviour.
Glory be…

Hail Mary
Full of Grace

Antiphon
The Holy Spirit will come upon you, Mary, and the power of the Most High will overshadow you, alleluia.

Benedictus (if said in the morning) or Magnificat (if said in the evening) - see inside back cover for these prayers

Intercessions
Eternal Father, through your angel you made known our salvation to Mary. Fill of confidence we pray:
℞ Lord, fill us with your grace.
You chose the Virgin Mary to be the mother of your Son; have mercy on all who await your redemption.
℞ Lord, fill us with your grace.
By the consent of your handmaid and the power of the Holy Spirit, your Word came to dwell among us; open our hearts to receive Christ.
℞ Lord, fill us with your grace.
To you, O God, nothing is impossible; save us, and on the last day, along with all the faithful departed, bring us to yourself.
℞ Lord, fill us with your grace.

Our Father…

Concluding prayer
Shape us in the likeness of the divine nature of our Redeemer,
whom we believe to be true God and true man,
since it was your will, Lord God,
that he, your Word,
should take to himself our human nature in the womb of the Blessed Virgin Mary.
We make our prayer through Christ our Lord.
Amen.

Hail Mary (Ave Maria)

Hail Mary, full of grace.
The Lord is with thee.
Blessed art thou amongst women, and blessed is the fruit of thy womb, Jesus.
Holy Mary, Mother of God,
pray for us sinners,
now and at the hour of our death.
Amen.

The Hail Mary or Ave Maria is a traditional Catholic prayer asking for the intercession of the Virgin Mary, the mother of Jesus and it forms the basis of the Rosary. The prayer is also used by other Christian denominations and most of its text can be found in the Gospel of Luke (i.e. Luke 1:28 and 1:42).

Hail Mary
Full of Grace

Wednesday - Visitation

Introduction

O God, come to our aid. Lord, make haste to help us.

Glory be to the Father and to the Son and to the Holy Spirit, as it was in the beginning, is now, and ever shall be, world without end. Amen. Alleluia.

Hymn

Queen, on whose starry brow doth rest
The crown of perfect maidenhood,
The God who made thee, from thy breast
Drew, for our sakes, his earthly food.

The grace that sinful Eve denied,
With thy Child-bearing, reappears;
Heaven's lingering door, set open wide,
Welcomes the children of her tears.

Gate, for such royal progress meet,
Beacon, whose rays such light can give,
Look, how the ransomed nations greet
The virgin-womb that bade them live!

O Jesus, whom the Virgin bore,
Be praise and glory unto thee;
Praise to the Father evermore
And his life-giving Spirit be.

Venantius Fortunatus 530-609
Tr R A Knox 1888-1957

Antiphon

Mary arose and went with haste to the hill country, to a city of Judah, alleluia.

Psalmody

Canticle 21(Ephesians 1:31)

Blest be the God and Father
of our Lord Jesus Christ,
who has blessed us in Christ
with every spiritual blessing
in the heavenly places.

He chose us in him
before the foundation of the world,
that we should be holy
and blameless before him.

He destined us in love
to be his sons through Jesus Christ,
according to the purpose of his will,
to the praise of his glorious grace
which he freely bestowed on us in the Beloved.

In him we have redemption through his blood,
the forgiveness of our trespasses,
according to the riches of his grace
which he lavished upon us.

He has made known to us
in all wisdom and insight
the mystery of his will,
according to his purpose
that he set forth in Christ.

His purpose he set forth in Christ
as a plan for the fullness of time,
to unite all things in him,
things in heaven and things on earth.

Antiphon

Mary arose and went with haste to the hill country, to a city of Judah, alleluia.

Hail Mary
Full of Grace

Reading
Joel 2:27-3:1

You will know that I am in the midst of Israel, that I am the Lord your God, with none equal to me. My people will not be disappointed any more. After this, I will pour out my spirit on all mankind, and your sons and daughters will prophesy.

Short responsory
℟ The Lord chose her. He chose her before she was born.
℣ He made her live in his own dwelling place
Glory be…

Antiphon
When Elizabeth heard the greeting of Mary she cried out with joy and said, 'Why should I be honoured with a visit from the mother of my Lord?' alleluia.

Benedictus (if said in the morning) or Magnificat (if said in the evening) - see inside back cover for these prayers

Intercessions
Let us proclaim the greatness of our Saviour who chose to be born of Mary; Confident that he will hear us, we ask:
℟ Lord, may your mother pray for us.
Sun of justice, you showed your day dawning in the Immaculate Virgin Mary; help us to walk in the light of your presence.
℟ Lord, may your mother pray for us.
Christ, our Redeemer, you made the Virgin Mary, the sanctuary of your presence and the temple of the Spirit; make us bearers of your Spirit, in mind, heart and body.
℟ Lord, may your mother pray for us.

Our Father…

Concluding prayer
Almighty, ever-living God,
you inspired the Blessed Virgin Mary,
when she was carrying your Son,
to visit Elizabeth.
Grant that, always docile
to the voice of the Spirit,
we may, together with our Lady,
glorify your Name.
We make our prayer through Christ our Lord.
Amen.

Hail Mary
Full of Grace

Thursday - Birth of Christ

Introduction
O God, come to our aid. Lord, make haste to help us.

Glory be to the Father and to the son and to the Holy Spirit, as it was in the beginning, is now, and ever shall be, world without end. Amen. Alleluia.

Hymn
A noble flow'r of Judah
from tender roots has sprung,
a rose from stem of Jesse,
as prophets long had sung;
a blossom fair and bright,
that all the midst of winter
will change to dawn our night.

The rose of grace and beauty
of which Isaiah sings
is Mary, virgin mother,
and Christ the flow'r she brings.
By God's divine decree
she bore our loving saviour
who died to set us free.

To Mary, dearest mother,
with fervent hearts we pray:
grant that your tender infant
will cast our sins away,
and guide us with his love
that we shall ever serve him
and live with him above.

Antiphon
Joseph and Mary, the mother of Jesus, wondered at what was being said about him.

Psalmody
Canticle 23 (Colossians 1:12-20)

Let us give thanks to the Father,
who has qualified us to share
in the inheritance of the saints in light.

He has delivered us from the dominion of darkness
and transferred us to the kingdom of his beloved Son,
in whom we have redemption,
the forgiveness of sins.

He is the image of the invisible God,
the first-born of all creation,
for in him all things were created,
in heaven and on earth, visible and invisible.

All things were created through him and for him.
He is before all things,
and in him all things hold together.

He is the head of the body, the Church;
he is the beginning,
the firstborn from the dead,
that in everything he might be pre-eminent,

For in him all the fullness of God was pleased to dwell,
and through him to reconcile to himself all things,
whether on earth or in heaven,
making peace by the blood of his cross.

Antiphon
Joseph and Mary, the mother of Jesus, wondered at what was being said about him.

Hail Mary
Full of Grace

Reading
1 John 4:9

God's love for us was revealed when God sent into the world his only Son so that we could have life through him.

Short Responsory
℟ The Lord has made known our salvation, alleluia, alleluia.
℣ He has revealed his saving power.
Glory be…

Antiphon
Glory be to God on high, and on earth peace among his chosen people, alleluia.

Benedictus (if said in the morning) or Magnificat (if said in the evening) - see inside back cover for these prayers

Intercessions
God our Father, we greet the birth of Jesus, our brother and Saviour. He is the Daystar from on high, the lightbearer who brings dawn to us, who wait patiently for his coming.
℟ Glory to God in the highest, and on earth peace among men.
His birth bound heaven and earth in harmony and peace; establish that peace among us today.
℟ Glory to God in the highest, and on earth peace among men.
With Mary and Joseph we rejoice in the birth of Jesus; may we welcome Christ as they did.
℟ Glory to God in the highest, and on earth peace among men.

Our Father…

Concluding prayer
God, our Father,
our human nature is the wonderful work of your hands,
made still more wonderful by your work of redemption.
Your Son took to himself our humanity, grant us a share in the godhead of Jesus Christ,
Who lives and reigns forever.
Amen.

Hail Mary
Full of Grace

Friday - Sorrowful Mother

Introduction

O God, come to our aid. Lord, make haste to help us.

Glory be to the Father and to the Son and to the Holy Spirit, as it was in the beginning, is now, and ever shall be, world without end. Amen. Alleluia.

Hymn

God, who made the earth and sky
and the changing sea,
Clothed his glory in our flesh:
Man, with men to be.

Mary, Virgin filled with light,
Chosen from our race,
Bore the Father's only Son
By the Spirit's grace.

He whom nothing can contain,
No one can compel,
Bound his timeless Godhead here,
In our time to dwell.

God, our Father, Lord of days,
And his only Son,
With the Holy Spirit praise:
Trinity in One.

From the Stanbrook Abbey Hymnal

Antiphon

As sharers in Christ's sufferings, let us rejoice.

Psalmody

Psalm 128 (129)

'They have pressed me hard from my youth,'
this is Israel's song.
'They have pressed me hard from my youth
but could never destroy me.

'They ploughed my back like ploughmen,
drawing long furrows.
But the Lord who is just, has destroyed
the yoke of the wicked.

'Let them be shamed and routed,
those who hate Sion!
Let them be like grass on the roof
that withers before it flowers.

'With that no reaper fill his arms,
no binder makes his sheaves
and those passing by will not say:
"On you the Lord's blessing!"

'We bless you in the name of the Lord.'

Antiphon

As sharers in Christ's sufferings, let us rejoice.

Reading

Colossians 1:24-25

It is now my happiness to suffer for you. This is my way of helping to complete, in my poor human flesh, the full tale of Christ's afflictions still to be endured, for the sake of his body which is the church. I become its servant by virtue of the task assigned to me by God for your benefit: to deliver his message in full.

Full of Grace

Short Responsory

℟ By the cross of her Lord stood Mary all-holy, queen of heaven and of earth.
℣ She won the crown of martyrdom without suffering the pain of death.
Glory be…

Antiphon

Rejoice, grief-stricken Mother, for now you share the triumph of your Son. Enthroned in heavenly splendour, you reign as queen of all creation.

Benedictus (if said in the morning) or Magnificat (if said in the evening) - see inside back cover for these prayers

Intercessions

Eternal Word, in the living flesh of Mary you found a dwelling place on earth; remain with us for ever in hearts free from sin.
℟ Lord, may your mother pray for us.
Christ, our Saviour, you willed that your mother should be there when you died; through her intercession may we rejoice to share your suffering.
℟ Lord, may your mother pray for us.
Loving Saviour, while hanging on the cross, you gave your mother Mary to be the mother of John; let us be known as her children by our way of living.
℟ Lord, may your mother pray for us.

Our Father…

Concluding prayer

God our Father,
when Jesus, your Son,
was raised up on the cross,
it was your will that Mary, his mother,
should stand there
and suffer with him in her heart.
Grant that, in union with her,
the Church may share in the passion of Christ,
and so be brought to the glory of his Resurrection.
We make our prayer through Christ our Lord. Amen.

Saturday - Assumed into heaven

Introduction
O God, come to our aid. Lord, make haste to help us.

Glory be to the Father and to the Son and to the Holy Spirit, as it was in the beginning, is now, and ever shall be, world without end. Amen. Alleluia.

Hymn
The ark which God has sanctified,
Which He has filled with grace,
Within the temple of the Lord
Has found a resting-place.

More glorious than the seraphim,
This ark of love divine,
Corruption could not blemish her
Whom death could not confine.

God-bearing Mother, Virgin chaste,
Who shines in heaven's sight;
She wears a royal crown of stars
Who is the door of Light.

To Father, Son and Spirit blest
may we give endless praise
With Mary, who is Queen of heaven,
Through everlasting days.
From the Stanbrook Abbey Hymnal

Antiphon
You have been raised up like the cedar of Lebanon, like the cypress tree on Mount Sion, O holy Mother of God.

Psalmody
Psalm 121(122)
I rejoiced when I heard them say:
'Let us go to God's house.'
And now our feet are standing
within your gates, O Jerusalem.

Jerusalem is built as a city
strongly compact.
It is there that the tribes go up,
the tribes of the Lord.

For Israel's law it is,
there to praise the Lord's name.
There were set the thrones of judgment
of the house of David.

For the peace of Jerusalem pray:
'Peace be to your homes!
May peace reign in your walls,
in your palaces, peace!'

For love of my brethren and friends
I say: 'Peace upon you.'
For love of the house of the Lord
I will ask for your good.

Antiphon
You have been raised up like the cedar of Lebanon, like the cypress tree on Mount Sion, O holy Mother of God.

Reading
Isaiah 61:10
I exult for joy in the Lord, my soul rejoices in my God, for he has clothed me in the garments of salvation, he has wrapped me in the cloak of integrity, like a bride adorned in her jewels.

Hail Mary
Full of Grace

Short responsory
℟ The Virgin Mary has been exalted high above the choirs of angels.
℣ Blessed is the Lord who raised her up.
Glory be…

Antiphon
See the beauty of the daughter of Jerusalem, who ascended to heaven like the rising sun at dawn.

Benedictus (if said in the morning) or Magnificat (if said in the evening) - see inside back cover for these prayers

Intercessions
Let us proclaim the greatness of our Saviour who chose to be born of Mary;
Confident that he will hear us, we ask:
℟ Lord, may your mother pray for us.
King of kings, you assumed Mary into heaven to be with you completely in body and soul; may we seek the things that are above and keep our lives fixed on you.
℟ Lord, may your mother pray for us.
King of heaven and earth, you placed Mary at your side to reign as queen for ever; grant us the joy of sharing in your glory.
℟ Lord, may your mother pray for us.
Father, may the dead enter your kingdom and rejoice with Mary and the saints for ever.
℟ Lord, may your mother pray for them.
May your Church be united in heart and soul, held fast by love; may your faithful be joined in continuous prayer, with Mary the mother of Jesus.
℟ Lord, may your mother pray with us.

Our Father…

Concluding prayer
Almighty, ever-living God,
you have taken the mother of your Son,
the immaculate Virgin Mary,
body and soul into the glory
where you dwell.
Keep our hearts set on heaven
so that, with her, we may share in your glory.
We make our prayer through Christ our Lord.
Amen.

Full of Grace

Supplementary
resources

- Quotes on Our Lady
- Outlines to Church Documents
- Marian Prayers, including a brief guide to the Rosary
- Mary and the Liturgical Year
- Shrines and Apparitions
- Bibliography

Hail Mary
Full of Grace

Quotes on Our Lady

Praise due to Mary, Mother of God
May the heart of Mary be in each Christian to proclaim the greatness of the Lord; May her spirit be in everyone to exult in God.

St Ambrose

What sort of gifts shall we offer her? O that we might at least repay to her the debt we owe her! We owe her honour, we owe her devotion, we owe her love…She, who is the mother of Christ, is the mother of our wisdom, mother of our righteousness, mother of our sanctification, mother of our redemption. She is more our mother than the mother of our flesh. Better therefore is our birth which we derive from Mary, for from her is our holiness, our wisdom, our righteousness, our sanctification, our redemption.

St Aelred of Rievaulx

Mary's motherhood, which becomes man's inheritance, is a gift: a gift which Christ himself makes personally to every individual… For every Christian, for every human being, Mary is the one who first 'believed,' and precisely with her faith as Spouse and Mother she wishes to act upon all those who entrust themselves to her as her children. The more her children persevere the nearer Mary leads them to the 'unsearchable riches of Christ' (Ephesians 3:8).

Pope John Paul II – Redemptoris Mater, 45-46

Immaculate Conception
Only you [Jesus] and your Mother are more beautiful than everything. For on you, O Lord, there is no mark; neither is there any stain in your Mother.

St Ephrem of Syria – Carmina Nisibena

Mary is full of grace, proclaimed to be entirely without sin. God's grace fills her with everything good and makes her devoid of all evil. God is with her, meaning that all she did or left undone is divine and the action of God in her. Moreover, God guarded and protected her from all that might be hurtful to her.

Martin Luther

Joachim and Ann (*parents of Mary according to Tradition*)
O blessed couple. All creation is in your debt. For through you it presented the noblest of gifts to the creator, namely a spotless mother who alone was worthy for the creator.

St John Damascene

Hail Mary
Full of Grace

Mary-Eve

Behold the world! To it were given two eyes: Eve was the left eye, the blind eye; the right eye, the luminous eye is Mary. Because of the eye that grew dark, the whole world became dark. Groping in the shadows, men will consider every stone on which they stumble to be a god. When the world shines once more, by the other eye, men will rediscover unity.

St Ephrem of Syria – Hymns on the Church

Jesus is fully human and fully divine

The evangelist clearly states that Christ came forth from the Virgin's body in these words: 'That which is conceived in you' (Matthew 1:20), and Paul does the same: 'Born of a woman' (Galatians 4:4), in order to stop the mouths of those who say that Christ passed through his Mother's womb as if through a channel.

St John Chrysostom – Homily on Matthew 4

Virgin Birth

Do not look for conformity with the natural order of things, since what has happened transcends the natural order… If she had not been a virgin, there would have been no sign, since a sign has to be something out of the ordinary and beyond the laws of nature, something new and unexpected, something that makes an impression on those who see it and hear of it.

St John Chrysostom – From his Homily on Genesis 49 and his Commentary on Isaiah 7

If the Son of God had wanted merely to appear, He could certainly have assumed any kind of body, even one better than ours. Instead it was our kind of body that He took. He took it from a pure and unstained Virgin. This body was pure and not corrupted by union with man. For since he is the All-powerful and the Craftsman of all things, He made for Himself a temple within the Virgin; that is to say, a body.

St Athanasius – On the Incarnation of the Word

Mary and the Most Holy Trinity

Oh ! I love you, Mary, saying you are the servant of the God whom you charm by your humility. This hidden virtue makes you all-powerful. It attracts the Holy Trinity into your heart. Then the Spirit of Love covering you with his shadow, the Son equal to the Father became incarnate in you.

St Thérèse of Lisieux

Adoration to the Father Who created thee! Adoration to they Son, Who took flesh from thee! Adoration to the Holy Spirit, Thy Divine Spouse! Three in One, One in Three. Equal in all things. To Him be glory for ever. For ever. For ever. Amen.

St Lomman, Abbot – The Praises of Mary

Hail Mary
Full of Grace

Mary's faith in her Son

Rightly should human pride be abashed on seeing God so abashed in the womb of the Virgin Mary, who was that sweet field in which was sown the seed of the Word Incarnate, the Son of God… This is what God truly did, by virtue of the heat and the fire of the Divine Love that He had for the human race, casting the seed of His Word in the field of Mary. O blessed and dear Mary, you have given us the flower of the sweet Jesus.

And when did this sweet flower produce its fruit? When there was grafted in her the wood by the most holy Cross: because then we received perfect life… Such was Mary's desire that she could not desire anything other than the honour of God and salvation of creatures. Such was Mary's immeasurable charity – that she was willing to become a ladder herself so as to place her Son on the Cross if there had been no other way to do so. And all this came about because the will of the Son had remained in her.

St Catherine of Siena

Petition to Mary's Immaculate Heart

Mary, Mother of Jesus, give me your heart so beautiful, so pure, so immaculate, so full of love and humility that I may be able to receive Jesus in the Bread of Life, love Him as You loved Him, and serve Him as You served Him, in the distressing disguise of the poorest of the poor. Amen.

Blessed (Mother) Teresa of Calcutta

The Living Bread

The Church gave us the living Bread, in place of the unleavened bread that Egypt had given. Mary gave us the refreshing bread, in place of the fatiguing bread that Eve had procured for us.

St Ephrem of Syria – Hymns for the Unleavened Bread

> The section overleaf provides a brief outline to the various Church documents which concern Mary, the Mother of God. Church documents vary in importance from Apostolic Constitutions, the most formal of documents, to Apostolic Letters. By far the most popularly understood form of Papal communication is the 'Encyclical' such as Pope John Paul II's *Redemptoris Mater* (Mother of the Redeemer).

Hail Mary
Full of Grace

Bulls and Constitutions

Ineffabilis Deus (Ineffable God) - 8 December 1854
In this key papal bull, Pope Pius IX defined *ex cathedra* the dogma of the Immaculate Conception of the Blessed Virgin Mary. The decree surveys the history of the belief in Christian tradition, citing the long-standing feast of the Conception of Mary as a date of significance in the Eastern and Western churches.

Bis Saeculari - 27 September 1948
This Apostolic constitution of the Sodality of Our Lady was promulgated by Pope Pius XII. It is important for the fact that Apostolic constitutions are the highest form of Papal teaching, above encyclicals, and below dogmatisation *ex cathedra*. The Sodality of Our Lady dates to 1584 and consists of associations of persons, sodalists, dedicated to a Christian life, following the model of the Virgin Mary.

Munificentissimus Deus (Most Bountiful God) - 1 November 1950
This Apostolic constitution, issued by Pope Pius XII, defines *ex cathedra* the dogma of the Assumption of the Blessed Virgin Mary. It is the second *ex cathedra* infallible statement ever made by a Pope, the first since the official ruling on Papal Infallibility was made at the First Vatican Council (1869-1870).

Papal encyclicals

Ad Diem Illum - 2 February 1904
This encyclical, by Pope Pius X, was given in commemoration of the fiftieth anniversary of the dogma of the Immaculate Conception. It is an important document because it explains the Mariology of Pope Pius X. In it he shows his desire for the restoration of all things in Christ (his motto was *Omnia restaurare in Christo*), to whom there is no safer or more direct road than Mary. To Pope Pius X, Mary unites all humankind in Christ.

Deiparae Virginis Mariae - 1 May 1946
This encyclical, issued by Pope Pius XII, was directed to all Catholic bishops on the possibility of defining the Assumption of the Blessed Virgin Mary as a dogma of faith, eventually leading to *Munificentissimus Deus* in 1950. For years numerous petitions were received begging that the bodily Assumption into heaven of the Blessed Virgin should be defined and proclaimed as a dogma of faith. This was also fervently requested by almost two hundred fathers in the First Vatican Council (1869-1870).

Hail Mary
Full of Grace

Ingruentium Malorum - 15 September 1951
This encyclical of Pope Pius XII focused on the Rosary and was issued on the Feast of the Seven Sorrows of the Virgin Mary. It entrusts to the Mother of God the destiny of the human family. He strongly suggests that Catholic families should pray the Rosary together and that while reciting the Rosary, Catholics should not forget those who languish in prison camps, jails, and concentration camps.

Fulgens Corona - 8 September 1953
This encyclical by Pope Pius XII was issued on the Feast of the Nativity of the Blessed Virgin Mary. The encyclical proclaimed a Marian year for 1954 and is significant as it contained the Mariology of Pope Pius XII.

Ad Caeli Reginam - 11 October 1954
This encyclical, issued by Pope Pius XII, established the feast of the Queenship of Mary. It states that assumed into heaven, Mary is with Jesus Christ, her divine son and should be called Queen, not only because of her Divine Motherhood of Jesus Christ but also due to her exceptional role in the work of our eternal salvation.

Redemptoris Mater - 25 March 1987
Pope John Paul II delivered this encyclical subtitled 'On the Blessed Virgin Mary in the life of the Pilgrim Church'. It focuses on Mary's role in the plan of salvation and in the Mystery of Christ. It also confirmed the title, Mother of the Church, proclaimed by Pope Paul VI at the Second Vatican Council on 21 November 1964.

Papal Apostolic Letters

Gloriosae Dominae - 27 September 1748
This Letter by Pope Benedict XIV refered to Mary as 'Queen of heaven and earth,' stating that Jesus has, in some way, communicated to her his ruling power.

Marialis Cultus - 2 February 1974
Pope Paul VI issued this letter subtitled, 'For the Right Ordering and Development of Devotion to the Blessed Virgin Mary,' clarifying the way the Roman Catholic Church celebrates liturgies that commemorate Mary and about Marian devotion.

Rosarium Virginis Mariae - 16 October 2002
Pope John Paul II issued this letter which emphasises total devotion to Our Lady and which views the Holy Rosary as a compendium of the Gospel message: 'The Rosary, though clearly Marian in character, is at heart a Christocentric prayer. In the sobriety of its elements, it has all the depth of the Gospel message.'

Hail Mary Full of Grace

Marian Prayers

Devotion to the Blessed Virgin began with the Archangel Gabriel's greeting 'Hail, full of grace' at the Annunciation and has continued throughout the Church's history. Prayers addressed to Mary do not imply any divinity on her part but rather they seek to take advantage of her role as the ultimate intercessor with her Son which began with her 'intercession' at the Wedding Feast of Cana.

Just as we offer prayers to God through His Son, our Lord Jesus Christ, so we offer our prayers to Jesus through Mary so that she may add her superabundant grace to them, making them more effective and acceptable to God.

Remember, O most loving Virgin Mary,
that it is a thing unheard that anyone
who fled to your protection,
implored your help,
or sought your intercession was left forsaken.
Filled, therefore with confidence,
I turn to you, O Mother,
Virgin of virgins,
to you I come, before you I stand,
a sorrowful sinner.
Despise not my poor words
O Mother of the Word of God,
but graciously hear and grant my prayer.
Amen.

Memorare

I am all yours, and all that is mine is yours, O Virgin, blessed above all.
Totus tuus ego sum, et omnia mea tua sunt, O Virgo, super omnia benedicta.

Totus Tuus - St Louis-Marie Grignon de Montfort

Hail Mary
Full of Grace

We fly to thy protection, O holy Mother of God, despise not our petitions in our necessities, but deliver us always from all dangers, O glorious and blessed Virgin.

Sub Tuum Præsidium

It is truly right that we bless you, O Theotokos, God-bearer, the ever blessed and most pure Mother of our God: more honoured than the Cherubim, and more glorious beyond compare than the Seraphim, for you, undefiled, gave birth to God the Word: therefore we praise you, O true Mother of God.

From the Liturgy of St John Chrysostom

Hail, thee, O most Blessed Virgin, Cause of our Joy! Through you has been repaired the curse of our first mother: through you we have received once more blessings of grace, adoption as children of God! Hail, O Virgin Mary – name most sweet! Hail, O Mother of God, most holy and most blessed! By the ineffable grace with which the Holy Spirit adored you as His Spouse and as the Mother of the Son of God, we beg of you to obtain from God the Son, that we, by the sanctification of that same Holy Spirit, become worthy Temples of His Glory. Amen.

St Andrew of Crete

The Angelus

The Angel of the Lord declared unto Mary.
And she conceived of the Holy Spirit.
    Hail Mary...
Behold the handmaid of the Lord
be it done unto me according to thy word.
    Hail Mary...
And the Word was made Flesh.
and dwelt among us.
    Hail Mary...
Pray for us, O Holy Mother of God,
that we may be made worthy
of the promises of Christ.

Pour forth, we beseech thee, O Lord, thy grace into our hearts; that, we to whom the Incarnation of Christ, thy Son, was made known by the message of an angel, may by his Passion and Cross, be brought to the glory of his Resurrection. Through the same Christ our Lord. Amen.

Angelus by Jean-Francois Millet (1814-75)

Hail Mary
Full of Grace

Mary, Mother of grace, Mother of mercy, protect me from the enemy and receive me at the hour of death.

Maria, Mater Gratiæ

I beg you, holy Virgin that I may have Jesus from the Holy Spirit, by whom you brought Jesus forth. May my soul receive Jesus through the Holy Spirit by whom your flesh conceived Jesus. May I love Jesus in the Holy Spirit in whom you adore Jesus as Lord and gaze upon him as your Son.

St Ildephonsus

The Angelic host, the race of men, all creation rejoices over thee, Mary, for thou art full of grace, a hallowed temple, a spiritual paradise. From thee, most glorious of virgins, our God took flesh; he who at the beginning of time was already God became thy child. He made thy womb his throne; he, whom the heavens cannot hold, found there his resting-place. All creation rejoices over thee. Glory be thine, Mary, for thou art full of grace.

St John Damascene

The Rosary

The Rosary (from Latin *rosarium*, meaning 'rose garden' or 'garland of roses') is a popular and traditional devotion. The term denotes both a set of prayer beads (see right) and the prayer itself, which combines vocal (or silent) prayer and meditation. The prayers consist of repeated sequences of the Lord's Prayer followed by ten Hail Mary's and a Glory Be; each of these sequences is known as a decade. The praying of each decade is accompanied by meditation on one of the Mysteries of the Rosary, which are events in the lives of Jesus Christ and his mother, the Blessed Virgin Mary.

The traditional 15 Mysteries of the Rosary were standardised, based on the long-standing custom, by Pope St. Pius V in the 16th century. The mysteries are grouped into three sets: the **joyful** mysteries, the **sorrowful** mysteries, and the **glorious** mysteries. The total number of Hail Mary's recited would equal 150 (the same as the number of Psalms in the Bible). In 2002, Pope John Paul II announced five new optional mysteries, the **luminous** mysteries, bringing the total number of mysteries to 20.

Jesus in Gethsemane by Sebastiano Conca (1676/80-1764)

Hail Mary
Full of Grace

The Joyful Mysteries
Said on Mondays and Saturdays, the Sundays of Advent, and Sundays from Epiphany until Lent

I. The Annunciation (Humility)
II. The Visitation (Fraternal Charity)
III. The Nativity (Love of God)
IV. The Presentation (Spirit of sacrifice)
V. Finding in the Temple (Zeal)

The Luminous Mysteries (Mysteries of Light)
Said on Thursdays

I. The Baptism of the Lord (Sacrament of Baptism)
II. The Wedding of Cana (Fidelity)
III. The Proclamation of the Kingdom (Desire for Holiness)
IV. The Transfiguration (Spiritual Courage)
V. The Institution of the Eucharist (Love of Our Eucharistic Lord)

The Sorrowful Mysteries
Said on Tuesdays, Fridays throughout the year; and daily from Ash Wednesday until Easter Sunday

I. Agony in the Garden (True Repentance)
II. Scourging at the Pillar (Mortification)
III. Crowning with Thorns (Moral Courage)
IV. Carrying the Cross (Patience)
V. The Crucifixion (Final Perseverance)

The Glorious Mysteries
Said on Wednesdays and the Sundays from Easter until Advent

I. The Resurrection (Faith)
II. The Ascension (Hope)
III. The Descent of the Holy Spirit (Zeal)
IV. The Assumption (Happy Death)
V. The Coronation of B.V.M. (Love for Mary)

1. *Make the Sign of the Cross and say the 'Apostles' Creed.'*
2. *Say the 'Our Father.'*
3. *Say three 'Hail Marys' while meditating on the virtues of faith, hope and love.*
4. *Say the 'Glory be to the Father.'*
5. *Announce the First Mystery; then say the 'Our Father.'*
6. *Say ten 'Hail Marys,' while meditating on the Mystery.*
7. *Say the 'Glory be to the Father.'*
8. *Announce the Second Mystery; then say the 'Our Father. Repeat 6 and 7 and continue with Third, Fourth and Fifth Mysteries in the same manner.*

Hail Mary
Full of Grace

Mary and the Liturgical Year

Feasts of Mary and related feasts (degree of importance, see key below)
readings for the day

December
8th - Immaculate Conception of the Blessed Virgin Mary (S)
Genesis 3:9-15, 20; Psalm 97:1-4; Ephesians 1:3-6, 11-12; Luke 1:26-38
12th - Our Lady of Guadalupe
25th - Nativity of the Lord - Christmas Day (S)
First Sunday after Christmas Day (or 30th) - Holy Family of Jesus, Mary and Joseph
Ecclesiasticus 3:2-6,12-14; Psalm 127:1-5; Colossians 3:12-21; Matthew 2:13-15,19-23 (A); Luke 2:22-40 (B); Luke 2:41-52 (C) - alternative, ad libitum, readings can also be found in the Lectionary

January
1st - Solemnity of Mary, Mother of God (S)
Numbers 6:22-27; Psalm 66:2-3,6,8; Galatians 4:4-7; Luke 2:16-21

February
2nd - Presentation of the Lord (F)
Malachi 3:1-4; Psalm 23:7-10; Hebrews 2:14-18; Luke 2:22-40 (shorter form 2:22-32)
11th - Our Lady of Lourdes (OM)
Isaiah 66:10-14; Jude 13:18-19; John 2:1-11

March
19th - Joseph, Husband of the Blessed Virgin Mary (S)
Samuel 7:4-5,12-14,16; Ps 88:2-5,27,29; Romans 4:13,16-18,22; Matthew 1:16,18-21,24 (or Luke 2:41-51)
25th - Annunciation of the Lord (S)
Isaiah 7:10-14, 8:10; Psalm 39:7-11; Hebrews 10:4-10; Luke 1:26-38

May
13th - Our Lady of Fátima (F)
31st - Visitation of the Blessed Virgin Mary (F)
Zephaniah 3:14-18 (or Romans 12:9-16); Isaiah 12:2-6; Luke 1:39-56

June
Saturday after Second Sunday after Pentecost - Immaculate Heart of Mary (OM)
Isaiah 61:9-11; 1 Samuel 2:1, 4-8; Luke 2:41-51
27th - Our Mother of Perpetual Help

Key: S – Solemnity; F – Feast; M – Memorial; OM – Optional Memorial

Hail Mary
Full of Grace

July
16th - Our Lady of Mount Carmel (OM)
Zechariah 2:14-17; Luke 1:46-55; Matthew 12:46-50
26th - Joachim and Ann, Parents of the Blessed Virgin Mary (M)
Ecclesiasticus 44:1,10-15; Psalm 131:11,13-14,17-18; Matthew 13:16-17

August
5th - Dedication of St Mary Major (OM)
Apocalypse 21:1-5; Judith 13:18-19; Luke 11:27-28
15th - Assumption of the Blessed Virgin Mary (S)
Vigil – 1 Chronicles 15:3-4,15-16,16:1-2; Psalm 131: 6-7,9-10,13-14; 1 Corinthians 15:54-57; Luke 11:27-28
Day – Apocalypse 11:19, 12:1-6, 10; Psalm 44:10-12,16; 1 Corinthians 15:20-26; Luke 1:39-56
22nd - Queenship of Mary (M)
Isaiah 9:1-6; Psalm 112:1-8; Luke 1:26-38

September
8th - Nativity of the Blessed Virgin Mary (F)
Micah 5:1-4 (or Romans 8:28-30) Psalm 12:6-7; Matthew 1:1-16, 18-23 (shorter form 1:18-23)
12th - Most Holy Name of Mary
Galatians 4:4-7 (or Ephesians 1:3-6,11-12); Luke 1:46-55; Luke 1:39-47
15th - Our Lady of Sorrows (M)
Hebrews 5:7-9; Psalm 30:2-6, 15-16, 20; Sequence (p.1190); John 19:25-27 (or Luke 2:33-35)
24th (England) - Our Lady of Walsingham
Galatians 4:4-7; Luke 1:46-55; John 19:25-27

October
7th - Our Lady of the Rosary (M)
Acts 1:12-14; Luke 1:46-55; Luke 1:26-38

November
21st - Presentation of Mary in the Temple (M)
Zechariah 2:14-17; Luke 1:46-55; Matthew 12:46-50

Note:
The principal Marian feasts in the Latin tradition, and the dogma they celebrate, owe their origin to the Church's declaration of faith in the Incarnation of the Christ. So we are therefore called to focus on the Blessed Virgin Mary wholly through her Motherhood of the Divine Son. The time par excellence for Christian people's Marian devotion, as Lambert Beauduin (1873-1960) once wrote, 'is the cycle of Advent and Christmas. For it is in the expectation of God's ancient people, at the manger, at Nazareth, in short in all the mysteries of the hidden life, that Our Lady appears to us in all the exaltation of her providential mission and in the shining light of her Divine Motherhood, in all her glories.'

Hail Mary
Full of Grace

Shrines and Apparitions

Our Lady of Lourdes (began on 11 February 1858, last on 16 July) in Lourdes, France by Bernadette Soubirous. Our Lady asked for prayer and penitence for the conversion of sinners and on the 25 February Bernadette was asked to dig in the ground and drink the spring water she found there. Our Lady told Bernadette that she was 'the Immaculate Conception'. Miraculous healings from the spring water. Bishop Laurence of Tarbes gave the declaration of approval on 18 January 1862. Between 4 and 6 million pilgrims travel to Lourdes annually.

Our Lady of Guadalupe (12 December 1531)on Mount Tepeyac, Mexico, by Juan Diego. Speaking in the local language of Nahuatl, Our Lady asked for a church to be built at that site. The Spanish bishop Fray Juan de Zumárraga told Juan Diego to ask the lady for proof. This she gave by providing the bishop with Castilian roses (not from Mexico and despite the winter) and an image on Juan Diego's cloak. Given the titles 'Queen of Mexico' and 'Patroness of the Americas', Our Lady of Guadalupe's basilica is the most visited Catholic shrine in the world.

Our Lady of Knock (21 August 1879) in Knock, co. Mayo, Ireland by several people aged 5 to 75. Our Lady appeared with St Joseph and St John the Evangelist. Behind them and a little to the left of St John was a plain altar on which was a cross and a lamb with adoring angels.

Our Lady of Fátima (6 apparitions on the 13th day of six consecutive months from 13 May 1917) in Fatima (Portugal) by Lúcia Santos and her cousins Jacinta and Francisco Marto. Our Lady identified herself as 'the Lady of the Rosary'. Prophetic messages regarding the conversion of Russia and possible world war. The reported apparitions at Fatima have been officially declared 'worthy of belief' by the Church.

The Miraculous Medal (Medal of the Immaculate Conception) was created by Saint Catherine Labouré following a vision of the Blessed Virgin Mary. Many wear the Medal believing it will bring special graces through the intercession of Mary if worn with faith and devotion.

Full of Grace

Main picture: Skyline of the Lourdes Basilica; Inset: Grotto of Massabielle

Our Lady of Beauraing (33 apparitions from November 1932 to January 1933) in Beauraing (Belgium) by Five children aged between 9 and 15. Our Lady stated that she was the Immaculate Virgin and at one of the last visions revealed her Golden Heart (hence the title Virgin of the Golden Heart) Approval came from the Holy See in 1949 under the direction of Bishop André-Marie Charue.

Our Lady of Lourdes at Carfin (1922) in Carfin near Motherwell, Scotland. Founded by Canon Thomas Taylor (author of 'The Little Flower' a book on St. Thérèse of Lisieux, the shrine's secondary patroness) after visiting Lourdes. Built during the Great Strike. Scottish national Marian shrine.

Our Lady of the Taper (1970) in Cardigan, Wales. Reviving a medieval devotion in 1956 Cardinal Griffin blessed a statue for the shrine, in 1970 Bishops Petit and Fox consecrated new church of Our Lady of the Taper. Designated Welsh national Marian shrine in 1986. Statue brought to Westminster in 2010 for Papal Visit.

Our Lady of Akita (1973) in Yuzawadai, near Akita, Japan by Sister Agnes Katsuko Sasagawa. Our Lady's messages emphasize prayer and penance, saying: 'Pray very much the prayers of the Rosary.'

Our Lady of Banneux (8 visions from 15 January and 2 March 1933) in Banneux, Belgium by Mariette Beco. Our Lady declared herself to be the 'Virgin of the Poor' and directed Mariette to drink from a local spring. Miraculous healings were reported. Recognition of the facts came from Bishop Kerkhofs of Liege in 1942 and definite approval came from the Holy See in 1949.

Hail Mary
Full of Grace

Left to Right: Our Lady of Guadalupe; Our Lady of Walsingham ; Icon of Our Lady of Częstochowa

Our Lady of Walsingham (1061) in Walsingham, Norfolk by Richeldis de Faverches. Lady Richeldis is taken in spirit to Nazareth and asked by Our Lady to build a replica of the Holy House of the Annunciation. The original shrine was destroyed at the Reformation. Pilgrimages began again after many years to the 'Slipper Chapel'. On 19 August 1934, the English Bishops named the Slipper Chapel the Roman Catholic National Shrine of Our Lady.

Our Lady (or the Black Madonna) of Częstochowa is both Poland's holiest relic and one of the country's national symbols. In it the Virgin Mary is shown as the 'Hodegetria' ('One Who Shows the Way') gesturing toward Jesus as the source of salvation. According to tradition it was St. Luke who painted it on a cypress table top from the house of the Holy Family. The Black Madonna is known as the Queen and Protector of Poland.

Our Lady of Willesden has according, to legend graced this ancient 'hill of springs' with both her presence and a holy well which dates from before AD 939. When, in 1954, Pope Pius XII established that every diocese should have a shrine for the veneration of Mary, Willesden was chosen in Westminster, her coronation taking place in Wembley Stadium in front of 94,000 people. The shrine dates back many centuries receiving a large number of pilgrims, including St. Thomas More.

Our Lady of Loreto refers to the Holy House of Loreto, in which Mary was born, the Annunciation occurred, and to an ancient statue of Our Lady found there. Tradition says that angels took the house from the Holy Land, and transported it to Tersato in 1291, Reananti in 1294, and finally to Loreto, Italy. She is patroness of people involved in aviation and construction. (See also pp.22, 25, 26)

Hail Mary
Full of Grace

Bibliography

naturally this bibliography cannot be considered exhaustive but serves as a useful starting point

Raymond E. Brown et al (Eds., 1978) *Mary in the New Testament*, Paulist Press International

Luigi Gambero (1999) *Mary and the Fathers of the Church: the Blessed Virgin Mary in Patristic Thought*, Ignatius Press

Luigi Gambero (2005) *Mary in the Middle Ages: The Blessed Virgin Mary in the Thought of the Medieval Latin Theologians*, Ignatius Press

Scott Hahn (2001) *Hail, Holy Queen: The Mother of God in the Word of God*, Doubleday

St Alphonsus Liguori (2000) *The Glories of Mary*, revised edition, Liguori Publications

Richard McBrien (1994) *Catholicism*, 3rd Edition, Geoffrey Chapman – chapter 30

Jaroslav Pelikan (1998) *Mary Through the Centuries: Her Place in the History of Culture*, Yale University Press

Karl Rahner (1963) *Mary, Mother of the Lord: Theological Meditations*, Herder & Herder

Joseph Ratzinger and Hans Urs Von Balthasar (2005) *Mary: The Church at the Source*, Ignatius Press

Fulton Sheen (1996) *The World's First Love: Mary, Mother of God*, Ignatius Press

Church documents (see also pp.52-3)

Lumen Gentium, chapter 8 – http://tinyurl.com/onthechurch

(1999) *Catechism of the Catholic Church*, Geoffrey Chapman – especially 487-511, 829 and 963-975

Compendium of the Catechism of the Catholic Church – especially 196-199
http://tinyurl.com/compcreed3

John Paul II (1987) *Redemptoris Mater* – http://tinyurl.com/motherofjesus

Hail Mary
Full of Grace

Notes

Hail Mary
Full of Grace